. . . this thing called

Life

POETRY BY
ANDREW SMITH

Kipekee Press
Hamilton, ON, Canada
kipekeepress.com
info@kipekeepress.com

ISBN paperback 978-1-990728-51-8
ISBN eBook 978-1-990728-52-5

Also by the Author

Rebuilding Janise:
A Family's First Year After A Stroke

POETRY

... a life in motion (in movement through time)
...in search of redemption: the journey of a lifetime

DEDICATION

To the Creator of All
All the things in my world
Both seen and unseen

The physical and spiritual
The mysteries of the mystical
What is known and unknown

I thank you
You have created ME

To a boy and a girl
Who met through chance
Had a natural attraction

Turned their love to a verb
Through penetrating interactions
That caused a Big Bang!

I thank you
You have created ME

To the drum and the bass
Developed in the Mother Land
Then spread throughout the world

Setting the pace of my movements
Adding rhythm to my life
I always check you for the time

I thank you
You have created ME

To the joy of LOVE
As I am lucky to have LOVED

To the Battles that have tested
The essence of who I BE

To the Losses that attempt
To break ME down

The ups and the downs
Comebacks and the turnarounds

I am here this day
Because I've learned from you

I thank you ALL
You have created ME

PRELUDE

awaken from sleep
before the sunrise
refreshed & anew
is the vibe

the perfect way
to start the day

first things first
to execute the plan
we move our bodies
we exercise

the perfect way
to start the day

the next step
is our nutrition
we feed our vessels
replenishing us

joined at the soul
our minds and our bodies
we are here to thrive
not just to survive

together forever
for the rest of our time

our sunrises & sunsets
& each and every night

the perfect way
to spend...
the rest of our days

#theperfectway

TABLE OF CONTENTS

CHAPTER 1

Loves

Loves

1. MY WORDS WILL REACH YOUR SOUL

So many words
At our disposal
Filling up books
Whole books of words

Safe words
Vetted and accepted
That navigate rooms
Useable in any situation

Forbidden words
Expressing ill will
Showing feelings...emotions
Exposing ourselves

The lines once drawn
They were so clear
Now it is so clear
That the lines are blurred

What once was right
Has devolved to be wrong
Our words are impacted
By the winds of change

Looking back at the past
With future eyes
Hindsight is twenty twenty
Can we correct past wrongs?

Yesterday's use
Of words today
Gives discomfort
Though the words are unchanged

Sticks and stones
May break our bones
But the use of words
May break our hearts

There's no test today
For a broken heart
And no way to know
When and if it mends

So I choose my words
First with my mind
And deliver them
Through my mouth with my heart

I take the time
To select my words
Though my words may still
Be used in error

I'll take that risk
Take a chance
In hopes that my words
Will reach your soul

2. DEEP & WIDE

Anticipation in the time before
Leads up to foreplay
Building unbearable tension
Then to The Act

Joy and bliss
Guilty wet pleasures
Deep & wide is the way
Affirmation of your openness

Encouraging each other
Giving and taking
Leading and following
Don't want this dance to end

We are in rhythm
Riding the same beat
Quarter, sixteenth notes and beyond
We goin' kill each other

Time is endless
And at the same time still
Our love is forever
As this Be our will

All things in this life
Must come to an end
As we reach our peak
Time & we come...we descend

Having climbed to the stars
The fall is great
We parachute into each other's arms
And land to the earth with grace

We give thanks to each other
And then to our God
For this gift so deep & wide
We received from above

3. LOVE

A strange phenomenon
But it's simply a thing
That you can possess and hold
And at the same time give

In addition it also
Gives an account
Will describe many things
Add context and feel

To me it's best use
Is in movement in action
Building and creating
Improving our lives

LOVE
A thing a description
An action
And ultimately just a word

Yet If I had my choice
Each and everyday
It would be
The first word heard

4. OUR HAIR

Nappy and knotted
Untameable and wild
Unprofessional and dread
Are some of what's been said

Yet when left alone
It grows high reaching for the sun
Or locked down it grounds us
To the earth where all life begun

Excluded from circles
Places and clubs
But we carve out our own places
And show it much deserved love

As be it afro or dread locks
Knotted braided or twists
Blown out to show out
Our hair has the right to exist

So celebrate it and love it
It's variety will meet your taste
I look on it with envy
As mine only grows below my waist

5. I AM YOUR KING
(AND YOU ARE MY QUEEN)

No need for you
To purchase tickets
And fly far and high
To support a lie

No need for you
To hear the news
And listen to pundits
Spew their views

No need for you
To watch the stations
And view visuals
Of a fake coronation

You've got a man
Who'll quench your thirst
Take care of you
And put you first

I am your king
And you are my queen
Together we are one
Will accomplish anything

Crowned years before
A union of love
Witnessed not subjected
And ordained from above

6. YOU SHINE

It is a warmth
Emanating out
From within

Guides you through
The difficulty
This harsh world
Can bring

A world with no promises
No favours to give
A world indifferent
To whether you give up or live

You've been through it
And moved past trials end
You know your value...your worth
A strong message you send

Now out from under anguish
And collecting yourself
Reflecting on self
Loving oneself

Yet through it all you maintain
A smile that blinds
Bright welcoming eyes
You truly do shine

7. ...SIMPLY USING THESE WORDS

I don't know your backstory
What motivates
Or is precious to you
But I can reach out and touch you

...simply using these words

Do more than just touch you
Hold and caress you
Build trust within you
Then undress and molest you

...simply using these words

I promise you will know me
And my truth which can be dirty
As I am open for you to see
Revealing all of my life story

...simply using these words

My goal is for you to see
Our strive for perfection is fantasy
And to be unafraid is truly free
So I am naked and raw for you to see

...simply using these words

8. THE ANSWER

More questions created
As each new sun arrives
But there is nothing truly new
Under the sun
From time on this earth
First begun

What will be done today
Has already been done
We are destined to repeat
The steps of those from the past
With hopes that our first steps
Continues our ancestors' last

Questioning past actions
That led us to this place
Wondering what our impact is
What difference have we made?
Has new ground been laid?

More questions than answers
Is what the wise will repeat
But there are those answers
That remove all questions
Those are the answers
That fit our intentions

You are the answer
That I've never questioned
Gave me a reason
And fulfilled my purpose

Gave me an abundance
Of drive and energy
So with each new sun
I live out my fantasy
As you gave me true LOVE
A home and a family

9. DOWNTOWN

I met you first uptown
You trusted me and guided me
Then took me to a town
When it was open
And I was down

Downtown
Exciting and new
A different world another place
With its spicy flavours
I developed brand new tastes

A site to be seen in the sun
But most beautiful when it rains
It'll wet your whistle and drench you
Wash away all of your pains

A wet and warm wonderland
An adult playground
Once you been there
You become free and unbound

I work for no one
I am my own boss
So I speak with this honesty
As I bear no cost

Yes I've given you
A lot to swallow
Another way to approach your LOVEs
For all your tomorrows

What I speak of is not nasty
Take a deeper look
Review my words
I speak only of a location
Despite what you think you've heard

Downtown a concept
A place a space where I belong
I visit it frequently
Because my absence
Could never last too long

10. WHEN YOU LOVE SOME 1

What do U do
When U L♥VE some 1
& they R no longer
That same some 1

When change comes 2 U
Each & every day
It becomes familiar
Like the new sun's rays

Life's choices take U
2 so many places
Through many roads
That U need 2 know

Giving U what
U need 2 testify
2 live in joy
& release the pride

So what U do
When U L♥VE some 1
Dig deeper in time
To when L♥VE 1st begun

U will C change
As part of it all

2 help U rise
After a great fall

2 make U grow
Beyond your reach
2 give U lessons
Only change can teach

So I take my time
& enjoy the ride
With U I have
L♥VE by my side

That's what U do
When U L♥VE some 1
& they no longer
R that same some 1

11. YOUR SPELL

Eye lusted 4 U
Since Eye saw U
Then U saw me

We were face 2 face

U turned around
2 walk away
Eye saw what shook

Then Eye was hooked

Pheromones hit hormones
We connected
& delved in 2 each other

2 within...from skin 2 skin
We explored & discovered
We were all over 1 another

Eye came

Out from within
But remained down under
Your spell

The way U carried yourself

It was your skin & your hair
It was also the way U smell

Eye marked U as mine
No pee was required
...or maybe just a little

Love is a tsunami
Comes in waves
...& not just as a trickle

So here we R
Decades in LOVE
Though Eye am not 1
2 kiss & tell

But we lust 4 each other
R still connected
& Eye remain down under

...your spell

12. YOUR SOMEBODY

We are not
Just anybody
To each other
We are somebody

Bodies that count
So much more than
Body counts

To be a count
Just another number
Monetizes love
& quantifies our slumber

We are not
Just anybody
To each other
We are somebody

Somebody
Each of us can count on
Somebody
To keep each other strong

We could have been
Anybody & anything

But we chose to be
Each other's everything

As the hours turn to days
Time appears and disappears
& as our days turn into years

We are not
Just anybody
To each other
We are somebody

13. WE FIT

We fit
every 1 can C
eye have always known

that eye fit
with U
around & in U

that 1st time eye saw U
eye was touched
then eye touched U

eye was breathless
then U spoke 2 me
through your soul

eye became speechless
when eye held U
when eye tasted U

eye do LOVE U
every 1 can C
& even smell it

every 1 nose
We fit
2gether...4ever

14. MY THING

I got this thing
I like to share
From time to time
It's my thing

It's been with me
For all my time
And I reveal it
When the time is right

It is quite big
So I take it slow
When I expose it
Expose you to it

Clothing is optional
No borders or walls
Leaving me naked
When you see it

Giving you pleasure
And a good dose of pain
Opening emotions
Your world flooding with tears

Making you question
Your every decision

Leaving you gagging
With no answers to give

But you will be freed
From your constraints
And opened up
From my reveal

You'll learn life
Is a series of moments
If missed, the thief time
Is up for the steal

You see
I got this thing
I like to share
From time to time

Poetry
...It's my thing

15. QUENCH OUR THIRST

Look at, NOT through, me
Listen & hear me

Take time to know me
Be with & support me

Hold & caress me
Feed & L♥VE (f**k) me

To quench my thirst

I will study & listen to you
Take the time to know you

Be with & uplift you
Hold & caress you
Feed & L♥VE (f**k) you

To quench your thirst

We can't win fighting one another
Our challenges must be faced together

It was through God we were joined together
With a union no one can put asunder

So we put each other first
To quench all of our thirsts

16. SISTERS

I've seen you
over the years
Walking this earth

Step by step
Hand in hand
& heart to heart

Together

Inseparable
Yet giving each other
The space
To be different

Contrasting personalities
& disagreeing perspectives
Yet joined at the heart

& at the soul

Life's victories
& It's wounds
Experienced together

Each having someone
To uplift & to scold

Each having someone
To back & to support

Each having someone
To love & to hold

Both fortunate
To have
A love like this

I am lucky
To witness
A love like this

17. POETRY TO UNLOCK EMOTIONS

These words & the occasional rhyme
Beats & rhythms
Breaks & syncopation
Unlock the door to emotions

Join me on a ride
Shotgun right by my side
Come with me on this odyssey
Where emotions have no limits
They are free to be

Tears & laughter will be exchanged
As we make our way through time & space
The g-forces of life's ebbs and flows
Will surely make us feel displaced

Before we start on our excursion
We will pray for a safe journey
Check that we have all we need
Check our bags that we have packed

Words & the occasional rhyme
Beats & rhythms
Breaks & syncopation
Poetry

...to unlock the door to emotions

18.   A WORLD WITHOUT YOU

Look over
But don't overlook
Judge
But don't prejudge
Rate
But don't underrate

Me

A grave mistake
You would regret
As I am someone
You can't forget

I promise You
That knowing Me
Has only added
To who You are

Imagine life
A life without
Another version
Of your world
How would your life
Be without

Me

There would be pools
Of bitter tears
Filling lakes
Flowing from rivers

No more rooms
Filled with joy
Or carefree laughter
Conquering pain

& My life
Could never be
Without
You

We fill the hole
The void we have
With each other
& our Love

You do for Me
& I do for You

& I could never
Be in a world
A world without
You

19. U MOVE ME

...& U move me

Always forward
Never backwards
My inspiration
& aspiration

U make me who
I must B

...& U move me

Open my eyes
Bring me 2 tears
Eye C U struggle
& not complain

U do what U
Must do

...& U move me

4 ever pushing
Setting my pace
Keep me in motion
& never stopped

Or allowing
Me 2 B
Still

What eye owe U
Cannot B paid
With paper currency
That man has made

Eye know your worth
U R priceless
2 my life

...& No 1 could ever
Take the place
Of U

Because
...U move me

20. I BELIEVE IN ME

Limitless potential
& endless possibilities
Driven by choices
Made each & everyday

Outside of the boundaries
Of my imagination
This is the playground
Where I choose to play

Beyond my reflection
As it restricts me
Not the only assessment
Of all that I see

Ready not waiting
To make my approach
At the verge reaching out
To who I could be

Posing the questions
& seeking the answers
Reaching locked doors
& knocking them down

Believing my instincts
Trusting my intuition
As my purpose is pure
& my judgement is sound

21. I AINT ALONE

I stand tall
Shoulders back
Chest forward
My head is high

I walk strong
Left foot right foot
Moving forward
With a steady gait

This world will test you
Change your road
From freshly paved
To dirt & mud

Have you struggling
Try to sink you
Get you stuck
& stop your stride

But I got an army
Not from a draft
Not subjugated
Only volunteer

Filled with people
From all the places

the diverse spaces
That I have been

They got my back
So don't f*ck with me
Cause if they find you
Payback is swift

They met with me
I saw them last night
At some BOOK LAUNCH
I was filled with love

They held me up
Encouraged me
Hugged me & loved me
We laughed & cried

We are together
On this journey
In this life
Until the end

They keep me standing
Keep me walking
Laughing & crying
& Filled with Joy

I aint alone

22. BECAUSE

Because every storm ends in calm
Because it is darkest before the dawn
Because we fought to do things right
Because it was right for us to fight

Because you are the matriarch
Because you are OUR Queen
Because your reign has come and gone
Because your glorious era has come to its end

Because we will be at your home going
Because that's what you would've wanted
Because life is way to short
...because WE LOVE YOU ♥

23. MY FAVOURITE 4 LETTER WORDS

foul yes i can be
rude absolutely
a likkle crass
yep...you can kiss all of my ass

very smart
yes always
twist you up
too easy

i do practice yoga
and breathe deeply
through every twist
bend and turn

vocabulary...extensive
but treat my peoples correctly
to avoid the onslaught
of my favourite 4 letter words

24. STILL HOLDING ON TO YOU

making each moment so special
arriving much too soon
then quickly going with your memories

there is not a single moment
not a tenth of a second
my mind will stray from you
stop running up on you

all i do is all i can
from all the things that i know
to help you reach your potential
and be all the things that you can be

yes the work is exhausting
it does prey on me
but i got my people
who do pray for me

when all has been said
when all has been done
i count on all of my blessings
to soothe all of my pain

blessed with your presence
you are still here with me
i am still loving up on you
i am still holding onto you

25. NASTY

The smell of your body
In the midst of a good sweat
The aroma of your essence
When your body is wet

It is this scent that enlightens
And inspires my very mood
The funk that motivates
And puts my needle into the groove

Many songs have been sung
Many words have been said
Chronicles of loves lost
And loves being found

The lyrics and words
Are clean and pristine
A love that is sanitized
Is not a love for me

Love is the dirt
The spots and stains
And ultimately
It is the smell that remains

So my love is messy
Raw and rough
Muddy wet and sticky
Never fancy

...my love is nasty

26. I LOVE THIS SH!T

You see I love this sh!t
It's why I do this sh!t
Much more than a want
It's become a need

It gives me life
It helps me breathe
And I love this sh!t
Because it is the sh!t

You'll get a glimpse
Into my heart
And in return
I'll touch your soul

But not before
I search your mind
Pull on your heart
And release your pain

It gives me life
It helps me breathe
And I love this sh!t
Because it is the sh!t

And when we part
You'll not be the same
No longer YOU
Totally rearranged

Now our connection
Is written in stone
Hard as a rock
And getting harder

Because we are free
To laugh and cry
With no walls to divide us
We can live 'till we die

It gives me life
It helps me breathe
And I love this sh!t
Because it is the sh!t

27.   I AM ME

I am the same
Wherever I am
No matter the space
Or the place that I be in

The disruptive change
I've always wanted to see
Surroundings have no impact
They can't change me

Consistent to a fault
Working on my flaws
Committed to my principles
Loving all that I am

My mouth can be foul
Yet my heart is clean and pure
My mind is always sober
With actions at times crazed

The disruptive change
I've always wanted to see
Surroundings have no impact
They can't change me

I am the same
Wherever I am
No matter the space
Or the place that I be in

28. THE ME IN YOU

Saying no to me?
Is saying no to who you think I am
You may know of me
But don't know in me what you will find

Take time it's yours
No need to spin and turn around
It's not your role
But that of the earth every single day

Much better when unforced
Clicking and joined
Not greased
Not rammed

And once inside
What you will find
Will shock your mind
With all the love that you'll discover

So say yes to me!
The you in me
That you will see
Will draw you to...

The me in you

29. IT STILL GETS HARD

From grade school
To higher learning
Marriage and children
And all of life's ups and downs

It still gets hard

When you are close to me
When I touch you and hold you
And I am enfolded
Within you

It still gets hard
For me to be away from you

It grows to this day
Raised up in the same way
As it did in days past
True stamina that lasts

It still gets hard
Drug and outside assistance free
With exercise and natural food in me
And you keeping me young and carefree

It still gets hard
For me to be away from you

And then it gets right to that point
Love will reach all of its limits
It will gush out through my pores
When I can no longer take no more

It still gets hard
But give me a little time
Just a little for some time to pass
For some rest and one more chance

It still gets hard
For me to be away from you

30. LOVE OF A LIFETIME

U know
it took all my life
2 find this LOVE
of a lifetime

eye have fallen
4 all that is U
yet eye am up
& remain standing

U got my LOVE
@ full attention
all the way up
& expanding

cannot resist
nowhere 2 hide
want 2 explore
all of U from the inside

willing & able
in this time – in this space
giving all of me
2 U in this place

together & forever
this promise we make
4 a lasting LOVE
'till we both meet our fate

U know
it took all my life
2 find this LOVE
of a lifetime

31. BEFORE I GO

My actions paint
Vivid pictures
That speak louder
Than anything you've heard

I work each minute
To the passing hours
To true-up the inner me
With the outside one you see

I am exactly
What you believe me to be
I have everything
All elements within me

Both the good and the bad
That you perceive
Are valid components
Of my personality

So love me or hate me
Acknowledge or ignore me
Or be somewhere in-between
It don't matter to me

I'm gonna be
The me I need to be
And for you
I wish the same

You'll find out
That before I go
You'll know who I am
And I won't say a word

32. WHAT'S MINE

What I need
And what I lack
Is within me to make
I will create

All I possess
In this world
Is only rented
'till the time I die

What's mine is mine
For me to have
And ain't got nothing
To do with you

So don't question why
What's mine is mine
You're stealing time
Away from you

There is work in this
Time and effort
Patience and restarts
That you're not privy to

All I possess
In this world
Is only rented
'till the time I die

What's mine is mine
For me to have
And ain't got nothing
To do with you

So let go all
Your run come
For the lump sum - I have
And all the questions as to why

CHAPTER 2

Battles

1. I AM NOT WHAT I WAS

I am not a victim
Of circumstance
Or a poor lost soul
Needing one last chance

I am not an addict
Of external remedies
Those compulsive pleasures
That bring instant ecstasy

I am not the reflection
Of the pain I've seen
And that which I've inflicted
On those I've been with

I am not the sum
Of what's been taken and given
Or a victim of the trauma
That I've been livin'

I am simply a man
Moving through his life
Tryin' to work shit out
And overcome my strife

In touch with my emotions
The joys the fears the full lot
Having truly reconciled
Who I am and who I am not

2. THE BEST ME

It has taken some time
The many miles of my journey
All those laps around the sun
From when my life begun

The triumphs and tear downs
All those lessons and learnings
Life's challenges and victories
Molded and created what you see

You see the ME from the past
Was a piece of work
Who needed life's tests
To move forward and progress

The pounding rhythms of my feet
Set the pace for my journey
It is this beat that would soothe
All of my deepest blues

So I stand here before you
With many scrapes and bruises
Balding with wrinkles and grey hairs
But with no wasted years

It is my great fortune
That what I have become
And what you are privy to see
Is truly the best ME

3. EASY

Easy?
It ain't suppose to be
No warranty or guarantee
A no return policy

Starting each day
From several steps before
Breaking through windows
When frustrated with locked doors

The freshly paved road
Ain't the one for you
Sweat and pain is the cost
And payment is due

Easy?
Not so fast
Can't sip from this sweet glass
And finally rest your ass

The hard way is your way
The work is here night and day
With eyes bloodshot it's hard to see
Rest is your only luxury

The lessons learned on the journey
Will be carried 'till times end
Be a continuous source
Of great power and force

Easy?
Perhaps this is our future
But for now we work...you and me
And that's how it will be

4. EVOLUTION

With each spin of this rock
As it rotates around our star
I find myself growing
Continuing to evolve

Reaching my destinations
Tirelessly working to arrive
Then in that instant
Moving on...continuing my stride

From childhood to youth
Teenager to man
Our stages have been scheduled
Part of a bigger plan

Though my spirited energy
Stays constant with each change
A calm confidence has been gained
With the knowledge that I can be anything

It's for us to learn
The lessons in each phase
And carry them and share
before we descend to our grave

Before we shed our vessels
And our spirit leaves to the divine
We must pass on our knowledge
To those we'll leave behind

What will you pass on?
If you never even changed
What could you have learned?
If you remained the same

With each spin of this rock
As it rotates around our star
Never stop growing
Make an effort to evolve

5. THE FOREIGNER

Not of this land
Or of any other
Of no fixed address
Lost and unknown

A wondering soul
Moving between worlds
Switching locations
When I've overstayed my time

I straddle cultures
An observer sitting on a fence
Feeling the sharp splinters
Painfully pinching my ass

Raised in this land
Reared on the culture of another
Their inconsistencies clash
Discord in need of resolution

On the outside looking in
A hybrid generation
A disrupter in all spaces
A foreigner in all places

6. LOST

I am lost in these surroundings
But a visitor...a guest
Here for the moment
But just passing through

A time traveller
From a different place
Somewhere from the past
Not as advanced as you here

Your people are plenty
Yet so many are lonely
They conceal their unhappiness
With the things they collect

Suffering mentally
Lacking real life connections
Using technology
To replace human touch

Spending their time
In a concrete maze
Running in a race
Created for a rat

Then realizing
The race has no meaning
But it's too late
Their grave is prepared

Y'all got the drugs though
For this situation
And food genetically modified
To make everything alright

It is my observation
We share one thing in common
We are lost
All of us

I have lost my way
...and you are lost in your ways

7. BELIEF

Much will be spoken
Much will be said
What you hold on to
Is what you believe

So take my name
Raise it high to the sky
Or drag it and hold it
Way down in the mud

What is most important
Is how I view me
And that I show up
As the person I L♥VE

Beliefs they are volatile
Can be high or be low
With the ebbs and the flows
Mimicking that of the tide

People are impacted
By their surroundings
Inhaling the wind
Of those with hot air

Much will be spoken
Much will be said
What you hold on to
Is what you believe

And what you believe
What you support
Can say more about you
Than it does about me

8. IMPERFECT

Our well thought out plans
Guided the journey
Moving with caution
We would abide by its steps

We did the right things
Created a strong foundation
Painted within the lines
Used our palette of colours

Then left wanting and yearning
Dissatisfied and disappointed
Angered and aggravated
Over the picture created

From the past to the present
Like the drunken driver
Weaving back and forth
Reliving our travels

Now searching for purpose
A hidden message to uncover
A reason for our current direction
A lesson in our imperfection

9. MY CUP RUNNETH OVER

At times I do get weary
Truly exhausted
But never tire

I am deep within the fog
With little clarity
In front of me

The steps I make are small
But they continue
To move me

My pace remains slow
But it does push me
Forward

I woke up on top of the earth
Not deep within
Six feet under

As life is in my possession
Both hope and faith
Will stay with me

It is the people in my life
Who always lift me
And hold me

Those close to me who
Support and comfort
And L♥VE me

I stay humble in my ways
Hopeful and thankful
And faithful

Though the days that are my past
Are so long gone
Behind me

Past lessons carried forward
Remain with me
And guide me

My plate in life is full
And my cup of blessings
Runneth over

It is my work that will lead
To goodness and mercy
Which will follow me

...for all of my days

10. LOST MEMORIES

We have made it this far
Together to this point
But your memories are out of reach
With a stroke our journey became unfam liar

Are your moments locked away?
Or deleted and removed?
I will lead the search...find the key
And bring the tools to restore you

All the things that it takes
Anything to make things right
To solve the puzzle that is you
Construct and rebuild your beautiful mind

11. THEY

They will tell you what to do
Have it all figured out
Exactly how you should live your life
Based solely on their own limitations

How dare you go against their rules
And create and break your own
Play outside their box...your imagination
Reaching levels
They dare not dream

Those who believe in you
And They who never will
Build
Strengthen and embolden
Your journey

Tragically
The role They play
To pull you down
Will result in their own stagnation

12. NOTHING

We start our lives
With plenty of it
And wish for the day
We want it

The paradox of our existence
Born with it
And only successful
When we want it

Nothing

With it
We can't do anything
Turning it into something
Makes us want it more

Nothing

Begins the race
Builds the drive
Feeds desire
For everything

We spend our time
Gathering and collecting
Become unfulfilled and empty
Numb...yet feeling

Nothing

To prove we are someone
We must show
That we have something
To everyone

The more we acquire
The more we need
Feeding the fuel that is
Our wants and our desires

Should we want more than
Each other
If we are to share this earth
Together

Nothing

Is what we need to have
For us to show LOVE and care
Towards
One another

13. MUSINGS OF THE CROWD

The choice to do
Something
Leaves me open
Exposed and vulnerable

To speculation
To the criticism and cynicism
Of those
That don't do

It is through actions
My endeavors
That I set an example
Which is revealed to the crowd

These same actions
Hold the key to my growth
Accompanied with the risk
Of my regression

Though the odds seem
Insurmountable
I discount them
As my purpose is clear
And my goal is pure

My ultimate success
Will disrupt
And abruptly interrupt
The endless
Musings of the crowd

14. THERE IS WORK TO BE DONE

It is what it is
And it ain't what it ain't
Not the result expected
There is work to be done

You have fallen down
You've been here before
Knee deep in this loop
Life repeats itself

Your spirit is strong
But your arm is broken
One step forward
And two steps back

Your back is fine
I've tried to break it
So many attempts
Over all of our years

I will not give up
And you the same
We both have our focus
Our focus is you

We know the plan
Let's take our time
As each of our steps
Brings us closer to our goals

It is what it is
And it ain't what it ain't
Not the result expected
There is work to be done

15. I AM NOT AN ISLAND

I am not a dependant
And normally not the one
To put my trust in people
Or things outside of me

I don't move in crowds
Or with the crowd's whims
I sail my own boat
And play captain and crew

I try not to bother
With things I can't control
Or be a bother to others
Everyone has their life to live

But I have been blessed
Held up and supported
Checked up on and checked
By unconditional L♥VE

Now open to receive
Help on my journey
No longer the one
Playing all of the roles

An independent man
Still plotting my route
But now accepting help
So I can stay the course

16. MY DEFINITION OF THIS MAN

Visible to the naked eye
But not in focus
A blur is what I will be

The more you blink
To clear your eyes
The less of me you will see

I can't fit into a box
Won't twist, bow or bend
Complying to the crowd
Is not a message I will send

I am not for everyone
Everyone is not for me

Consumable in small bites
Take the time
You may like what you see

I am simply a product
Of the life I've lived
Empathetic to
Yet cautious of
Who I let in

So draw on your life
And you may understand
This person who stands before you
The definition of this Man

17. LESSONS FOR MY SONS

i have learned to yield
when it is the right call
there is no purpose in triumph
when there is nothing to gain

i am not without flaws
of them i have lost count
they will never control me
but i don't count them out

i think then i act
keeps my head on my shoulders
& i only process thought
Through my head...on my shoulders

i have been given a voice
in which i use to speak
the ups & downs of a life
& lessons i choose to teach

i know words have power
to lead & direct
can enhance & degrade
any given situation

so use words that give life
uplift & energize
be in situations that feed you
give you the space to thrive

set your targets high
to shoot for the stars
work for what you earn
& never change who you are

18. MESSY AND DUTTY

messy and dutty

nasty and rude
foul and hurtful
is what this life could be

taking kindness from others
and mistaking it as weakness
is a miscalculation
compromising relations

our eyes only see
as far as the surface
can't possibly visualize
what makes up our insides

so I don't poke no bears
or tease any lions
cause f*cking around
makes you find out

and things could get
messy and dutty
nasty and rude
foul and hurtful

...but this ain't how we should be

19. THAT DAY

Because it happened that day
I can't forget that day
My world forever changed
My life never the same

You fell down that day
Did not wake that day
I have yet to stop crying
My soul is still healing

The old me died that day
I was reborn that day
My life took on new meaning
With you as my "soul" purpose

I felt true loss that day
I was so lost that day
What purpose does life serve
If I am to serve it without you

I learned to write that day
Showed my true self that day
I became transparent
And used my pain as a superpower

It is because of that day
My tears that flowed that day
Every time I feel some joy
My laughter slows...
Stops
Then I cry

I learned so much that day
I was so strong that day
Everything this life throws me
I receive learn and release it

I am at peace this day
Unbreakable this day
There is so much love around me
People to hold me up and ground me

It is because of that day!

20. THE CHOICE IS YOURS

Eggs have been broken
And tea has been spilled
Can we go back to a time
Before this mess was made

To keep this very feeling
Would continue the shame
Exchanging sharp stares
That transports the blame

Only the will is needed
To review opposing views
To break free from this way
Breaking chains to start anew

It is for us to decide
Can't put this on God
Who watches from great seats
With a bowl of popcorn

If it is to be done
It won't be the same
We've passed through life's fire
And we have been changed

We are no worse or better
From our state before
Perhaps with hearts that are open
And cracked windows and doors

This - not a poem but an offer
Or better yet a branch
From the tree of an olive
Or the stem of a rose

It could moisten and soothe you
And soften your skin
Or cut you with thorns
For blood letting to begin

This life is a risk
Filled with many choices
That's what we are here for
So the choice is yours

Backwards or forward
The past or the future
The choice is yours
The choice is yours

Eyes wide open
Or closed real tight
The choice is yours
The choice is yours

Stay in the darkness
Or move toward the light
The choice is yours
The choice is yours

21. WORDS

Words have meaning
Each one of them
They are heavy
Should never be taken lightly

Our word is our bond
Connecting us to each other
Forms the foundation of
How we relate to one another

Words can be creative
When created from the behind
But prematurely ejaculates
Avoiding the long trip to the mind

These words come with a stench
It can't be happenstance
The strongest odour emanating
Is that of ignorance

Flippant conversations
Leave listeners in the dark
As to true intentions
The meaning behind remarks

Words have meaning
Each one of them
They are heavy
Should never be taken lightly

If your words are empty
& have no real meaning
It is better that you simply
Cease-and-desist

Don't play with words
It is a serious thing
As words are the source of
The creation and destruction of everything

22.   I SAID WHAT I SAID

I said what I said
It has already been done
No take backs no do overs
Life cannot be redone

It can replay in your mind
Thousands of times
But the result will remain
The ending the same

You can torture your soul
With only the past being viewed
Or be present in this time
Beginning this day - start anew

If it's sorry you need
Then sorry you will be
The truth don't ride shotgun
With sympathy and empathy

Come out of your feelings
Try to find some sanity
Your anger and pride
Has no impact on reality

I said what I said
It has already been done
No take backs no do overs
Life cannot be redone

23. MORE

there is more
U are not
one thing

2 find more

seek more
feel more
and U will be more

24. THOSE WHO ENDURE

Our risks are calculated
Our confidence cocksure
We keep striving for answers
Constantly pushing for much more

Satisfaction is a moving target
With no promises or guarantees
The closer we do get to it
The further away that it feels

Working as one body and mind
Intertwining our hearts and our souls
Maintains our movement forward
And drives us towards our goals

Though there's no immediate solution
And we have no quick cure
But we are here for the duration
This is the battle we must endure

25. TRUE FREEDOM

Here I stand within the borders
Of a foreign land
Chased by an army
Led by the forces of Babylon

Now deep within
The belly of this beast
My movements are calculated
And so is my speech

But my thoughts and my feelings
Are as free as the wind
So despite this despair
I walk around with a grin

You can capture the body
With the mind still unchained
The vessel is but the physical
The higher level is my plain

Where the I remains

The lesson to learn
Is that of the physical is hollow
True freedom starts with your mind
Your ass will have no choice but to follow

26. DAY BY DAY

I will rumble in your jungle
Even fight in your ring
I will be Ali to your Foreman
& always finish with the win

Day-by-day is where the work is
Time's not my enemy, it's my friend
Taking in everything that comes at me
And staying in control 'till the end

As graceful as a butterfly
But the bee in me will sting
Rope-a-dope, bob and weave
With constant energy as when I begin

Though the days months and the years
Become indistinguishable from one another
Quieting the noise and slowing the flow
Keeps my focus aligned to where it should go

I will rumble in your jungle
Even fight in your ring
I will be Ali to your Foreman
& always finish with the win

Day-by-day is where the work is
Time's not my enemy it's my friend
Taking in everything that comes at me
And staying in control 'till the end

27. DISCOVERY

I am finding the wins
Within the losses
And weighing the benefits
Against the costs

What we lose
Is an inescapable fee
But the lessons learned
Can provide us with the key

To the doors of possibilities
Opening hallways of hope
That supersede our pain
And give us strength to cope

With this life
And it's terminal disease
It's contusions and bruises
And scars that reopen and bleed

I make the best of my cards
Found myself and I stayed true
With each battle I am faced with
I have the will to push on through

28. EVERYONE, EVERYWHERE, EVERYPLACE

Pain and loss
Sadness and despair
Takes its victims by surprise
Leaving them unaware

There is not one of us
Who is truly safe
From its arms and its reach
Which will search out and seek

Everyone
Everywhere
Everyplace

A one-sided contract
That you did not sign into
But have been signed on to

Not fair in its distribution
But always fair in its inclusion
And its promise to touch

Everyone
Everywhere
Everyplace

In this cruel world
These things remain just
Having consistent actions
Though unequal and prejudicial

There are no sides
They choose to take
The fence is where they sit
In the attempt to find and hit

Everyone
Everywhere
Everyplace

29. THINGS YOU DON'T NEED

it is our most
yearning desires
when fulfilled
can feel empty

joy when short-term
its feeling is fleeting
will leave you wanting
hollow & lacking

leaving you stuck
deep in confusion
unable to distinguish
your needs from your wants

this is the time
to maintain your focus
and stay true to you
stay true to your purpose

take the time
to take care of you
to learn what you're meant for
and what you should strive for

because
all that you want
comes with things
you don't need

CHAPTER 3

Losses

Losses

1. WHEN YOUR WORK IS DONE

When your work is done
It is time to rest
Sit back and reflect
Count your spoils and your blessings

You have hunted and gathered
For near all your life
Raised a loving family
After you found you a wife

When your work is done
You are surrounded by family
Children and grands
That came up from your hands

The sun has set
As have your days
But the pain of this life
Will no longer block your way

You have transitioned
Been carried away...moved on
The memories you've left
Will be with us so long

Rest in peace with the angels
Look down and enjoy the view
What you will see from your vantage
Is a reflection of you

...as
Your work is done

2. FRACTURED

Fractured
Broken a little
But aren't we all
Just a little broken

Tried and tested
By this life
We know a fall is coming
And brace for it

Despite our best efforts
To make it soft
& not take the full impact
Sometimes we end up

Fractured
Broken a little
But aren't we all
Just a little broken

Down but not out
Resting but not taking comfort
As there are many steps to take
So many more miles yet to travel

At this time
We take our time
Be present in time
& not waste our time

Rest & recovery
From the journey
Is as important
As the journey itself

So yes...fractured
Broken a little
But aren't we all
Just a little broken

3. TRAUMA

It's not something to own
Lease or rent long-term
Trauma belongs to no one
And keeps no friends

It has plenty of company
As it is generous to a fault
Leaving all those it touches
Both empty and lost

A trail of bodies
In misery and pain
A legacy of victims
With shame and self-blame

Directing its followers
Down a dead-end path
Surviving and thriving
In pain's aftermath

Trauma is a tunnel
You must go through
A bridge or bypass
You must get past

It's not something to own
Lease or rent long-term
Trauma belongs to no one
And keeps no friends

To overcome the past
Requires your presence
To build a proper future
And be free of trauma's grasp

4. JUMOKE (EVERYONE LOVES THE CHILD)

Jumoke
Olajumoke
Was your name
Is your name

Yoruba origins
With meaning
Meaning
Everyone loves the child

Jumoke...our daughter
You were loved
You are loved still
Though you were still born

You were born...still
& created from love
So much so that you were called
Called back to love

We miss you
& missed out on seeing
The Miss or the Mrs.
You would become

You left us for the Creator
Who needed you more
Much more than us
You were needed

Needed by the side
The side of love
To do the work
The work of love

Jumoke…"me did dream you"
"Me mind did run pon you"
Wondered about you
& still caring about you

Jumoke
Younger sister of Jelani
Jumoke
Older sister of Jabari
& daughter of Janise & Andrew

5. WHAT IS GOOD

What is the good of eyes
If they are not being used
Intentionally blinded
To the wrongs that they see

What is the good of a nose
When it is numb to the odour
Of selfishness and wickedness
Gluttony and greed

What is the good of a mouth
That only spews lies
A lie-in-all the words
Camouflaged as ignorance

To be a witness and silent
Is to be an accomplice
In this case doing nothing
Is really doing something

There is no neutrality in life
There are positions to take
Between right and wrong
Protecting the weak against the strong

If your goal is to be loved
And charm-main-ly for the likes
You will stand for nothing...no one
And fall for all that comes at you

What is the good in a life
Lived only for oneself
What is the good in a life
Lived without community

NOTHING!

6. THE HUSH

Yes there is now a peacefulness
A calmness and stillness
A general quietness
That encompasses you...engulfs you
& surrounds you

The HUSH!

It has replaced the pandemonium
The mayhem and turbulence
The overall madness
That called me to you...attracted me to you
& captured me
For you

But I would be a damned fool
Practicing negligence
& filled with nonsense
Out of touch with my senses
Inattentive to you...blind to you
If I could not truly see
The essence that is you
Remains

The HUSH!

It has bent & buckled
It has truly tested
& It has slowed down
You & me

The HUSH!

Will never split or break
Will never separate
& will never ever stop
You & me

7. GOODBYE

the news came to me
through the grapevine
the ancestors called you
it was your time

you have joined them
June 21st the date
your table was readied
they set your plate

you have transitioned
we are left behind
empty and broken
losing you is a CRIME

but there is no gain
prosecuting the past
your vessel has perished
but your memories will last

the sound of your singing
when your cooking would start
the heavenly aromas
food prepared from the heart

the fear of grown men
the poor fools never knew
playing you in dominoes
was the wrong thing to do

we'll send you home properly
this is now our fight
not rest 'till your soul
has been truly done right

we'll take care of your memories
call your name out LOUD
we'll never forget you
live our life to make you proud

I'll take care of your daughter
your grandchildren too
be a guide to our family
do just what you would do

the news came to me
through the grapevine
you are an ancestor
it was your time

8. GONE HOME

You have gone home
On this very day
Your worries and pains
Have faded away

So sad was the day
It was confirmed to be true
Unforgettable the moment
That we all finally knew

We travelled we did
From near and far
Moving mountains and time
To get to where you are

Now happy and content
Greeted by our ancestors
In the arms of pure LOVE
Seated with our Creator

You have gone home
On this very day
Your worries and pains
Have faded away

9. YOU GO YOUR WAY

For now
You go your way
And I'll go mine
The prescription we need
Is space and time

Space between us
And time to reflect
To dissipate hard feelings
That made us upset

It would be hard to forget
How we got to this place
Or if we can solve this
With a little time and some space

It is the best option
That we have stumbled upon
As the forest is ablaze
And the fire rages on

Time will offer
Our minds a rest
Space will expose
What we've lost
the void to address

For now
You go your way
And I'll go mine
The prescription we need
Is space and time

10. TO CATCH A THIEF (PART I)

taking it all and never giving
swallowing most of everything
sucking up all there is to suck
always stretching and pushing their luck

actions unchanged left on repeat
till cupboards are cleaned cleared and bare
when nothing is left and all is spent
they beg forgiveness but never repent

the thief in the night playing a victim's role
everyone else will pay their toll
pissing on all and calling it rain
the thief runs away to avoid the blame

but the sun will shine to scare the night
exposing actions to bright daylight
for all to recognize and witness the beef
It will take the light to catch a thief

11. TO CATCH A THIEF (PART II)

prayer and love will help us act
to expose the lies and reveal the facts
patience and time is what we need
all play a role and will help us succeed

we now do what we are forced to do
this why I now write
"to catch a thief part ii"

the real power in life is the word
It relays the stories of events that occurred
reveals the wolf cloaked as the lamb
the evil acts of those who are damned

a damned shame that it's come to this
but good that our weapons are words and not fists
at the end your name will be synonymous with doo doo
the result of your words and the things that you do

prayer and love will help us act
to expose the lies and reveal the facts
patience and time is what we need
all play a role and will help us succeed

we now do what we are forced to do
this why I now write
"to catch a thief part ii"

12. I AM AT PEACE (PART I)

My way is to release
So I can be at peace
Because I've said my piece
Now I am at peace

Tension it will build
And pressure it will rise
Testing who we are
And our will to survive

Working through this time
Can build your character
But the opposite can be true
Tension and pressure can break you

First moving slowly
Silent and deep inside
And will manifest itself
When it impacts your health

You must find a way
To get it out the way
I address it right away
To make it through my days

My way is to release
So I can be at peace
Because I've said my piece
Now I am at peace

13. I AM AT PEACE (PART II)

Life leaves room for everything
All things have time and spaces
We need to laugh and also cry
Make noise and find quiet places

We must know of the time
What to do and what it is
To hold our punches or push right through
Clench tightly or release our fists

The battle in the heat of war
Provides conflicts to overcome
The wounds and scars remind us of
Where we've been and where we're from

Life leaves room for everything
Pay attention at all times
Stay awake to the lessons dropped
Be aware of all of the signs

I stay at peace throughout my travels
It is needed each and everyday
It is not to be saved for a destination
But for strength along the way

Through my nose I breathe deep and slow
Clearing my thoughts sets my mind at ease
Allowing my breath to be my focus
Reconnects me to my peace

14. WHAT WE ARE HERE FOR

We are all here together
There must be a rhyme or reason
That we are here at this moment
But what are we here for?

We are visible I am quite sure
But we don't see one another
As we pass by our sisters and brothers
Dismissing and neglecting each other

We cannot truly care for others
Before we do so for ourselves
Learn to love the full naked natural picture
Reflected back from our mirror

It is to choose love over fear
To place the group above one self
To redefine success and wealth
That's what we are here for

15. FOR A TIME

Because you are here for a time
Make the best of your time
And take all of your time
To learn from your time

As we move through life
Our losses accumulate
Challenging us to survive and thrive
Finding ways and means to rejuvenate

Losses they can burden you
Weigh you down forever
You must bear them so make the choice
To carry them as light as a feather

Holding on to what you need
And dropping all the stuff you don't
All that which you have found
That will slow your progression down

Because you are here for a time
Make the best of your time
And take all of your time
To learn from your time

16.   WHEN I DIE / ALIVE

When I Die

People will run out of tears
In memory of their great loss
Tears will slowly turn to laughter
As they reflect and rejoice on the life that was

Flower shops will have to close
Sadly, unable to supply
The demand for petals
To be laid upon me

Places of worship will close their doors
Crowded, overflowing
No more room
To fit the people in

When I Die

Words so amazing
Will be spoken
With ME in mind
Through speeches, songs and the occasional rhyme

Pictures, slide shows and videos
Will be shared by onlookers
On the tragic news
And up to the day the people

Bury me and send me HOME
Never realizing...

I needed their tears
I needed their laughter
I needed their flowers
I needed the overflowing rooms of people

The speeches
The songs
The occasional rhymes
The support and company

When I was Alive

One thing I do know
It is of no use to me

When I Die

Alive

That's when I need you
When I am here
Not when I am gone away
Not tomorrow, but for today

Alive

Of this moment
I am sure

That your company is what is needed
It IS my cure

Alive

Cause someday I won't be
...to be is what I am now
But to not be
Is what I will be

So I only have, one ask
Not for the future
Not for the past
For the here and now

Make me your first, not your last
Priority
Thought
Action and love

Before i take my last breath
My last heartbeat
Before I...
Die

While I am accessible
You to me
And me to you
While I am...

Alive

EPILOGUE

Savour each moment
All that is experienced
The Loves
The Battles
And the Losses

Each gives you something
To take with you
To learn
About the people who surround you
About YOU

In
...this thing called life

We got this crack at it
A chance to make the most of it
Leave no stone unturned
And if you've missed a stone
Don't dwell on it

Opportunities cycle back around
In different forms
And can turn your world around
Worries and regrets are a waste
Wasted effort and wasted time

In
...this thing called life

We break down to rebuild
Ourselves - Each Other
Live a life in motion
Through our movement in time

Tread through this physical world
On a mission
In search of redemption
The journey of a lifetime

In
...this thing called life

We are on a one-way street
One way in and one way out
No one makes it out of this alive
So I have made up my mind
Made my choice to...

Savour each moment
All that is experienced
The Loves
The Battles
And the Losses

Each gives me something
To take with me
To learn
About the people who surround me
About ME

In
...this thing called life

#thisthingcalledlife

ABOUT THE AUTHOR

Andrew Smith is a loving husband, father, certified professional accountant and chartered account. He is also an author and speaker. He is known for his loud, infectious, evil-villain-esque laugh which goes well with his rambunctious sense of humour.

It is his insane humour that keeps him grounded as he navigates through the world. He continually aims to seek more, see more, feel more, and BE more. . . . *this thing called Life* is his fourth book.